LifeTimes

The Story of Mother Teresa

by Stewart Ross
illustrated by Victor Ambrus

Thameside Press

Distributed in the United States by
Smart Apple Media
1980 Lookout Drive
North Mankato, MN 56003

Text copyright © Stewart Ross 2001

Editor: Steve White-Thomson
Designer: Simon Borrough
Language consultant: Norah Granger, Senior Lecturer
  in Primary Education at the University of Brighton, U.K.
With thanks to Kay Barnham for her editorial help
  in the latter stages of this book.

Library of Congress Cataloging-in-Publication Data

Ross, Stewart.
  The story of Mother Teresa / written by Stewart Ross.
    p. cm. -- (Lifetimes)
  Includes bibliographical references (p.) and index.
  ISBN 1-930643-21-7
    1. Teresa, Mother, 1910---Juvenile literature. 2 Missionaries of Charity--
Biography--Juvenile literature. [1. Teresa, Mother, 1910- 2. Missionaries of
Charity. 3. Nuns. 4. Missionaries. 5. Women--Biography. 6. Nobel Prizes--
Biography.] I. Title. II. Lifetimes (North Mankato, Minn.)

  BX4406.5.Z8 R67 2001
  271'.97--dc21
  [B]   2001027186

Printed in Hong Kong

9 8 7 6 5 4 3 2 1

Introduction

Agnes Bojaxhiu was born in Skopje, Albania, in 1910 to a Roman Catholic family. At the age of 18, Agnes decided to become a nun. This would mean spending the rest of her life in the service of God.

Agnes joined the Loreto nuns and took a new name – Teresa. In 1931 she was sent to India as a teacher.

Our story begins 13 years later, when Sister Teresa was teaching English at St. Mary's High School in Calcutta…

Through the Window

"Nirmana," said Sister Teresa kindly, "do you know what 'charity' means?"

Nirmana loved her teacher and did not want to let her down. But she spoke Bengali at home, and her English was not very good.

"Is it… help for poor people?" she asked.

"It is," smiled Sister Teresa. "Now, can you tell me a word which means the same as charity?"

On the blackboard:

Charity.
α Love

"I think charity is love, Sister. When you love people, even poor people, you will help them."

"Well done, Nirmana!" replied Sister Teresa. She asked the class to write the words "love" and "charity" in a sentence, then walked slowly over to the window.

Beyond the school wall, she could see the slum area known as Motijhil. Thousands of the city's poorest people lived here, many without shelter. Motijhil was a sad place of disease, pain, and loneliness.

As Sister Teresa gazed at the slum, she remembered Jesus' words – *Blessed are the poor.* Should I be teaching these girls? she thought. Or do the people of the slum need me more?

Sister Teresa sighed and turned back into the room. If only she knew what God really wanted her to do…

When a woman becomes a nun, she takes three vows – poverty, chastity, and obedience. The nun promises that she will not have money of her own, not marry or have children, and always do as she is told by a senior nun or priest.

Obedience

Every day Sister Teresa asked for God's help
in her prayers. Was she doing enough for
the very poor? She received no answer.

God is testing me,
she thought. If I am
patient, he will
show me a sign.

One hot afternoon two years later,
Sister Teresa was asked to see Mother Cenacle,
head of St. Mary's High School.

"I have something important to discuss with
you, Sister," the elderly nun began. She looked
at Teresa for a moment or two and sighed. The
poor woman seemed absolutely exhausted.

"First, I want to thank you for all your help,"
Mother Cenacle said quietly. "I don't know
where I'd be without you."

"I am only doing my duty," replied Sister Teresa humbly.

"Of course. But what else are you doing apart from your duty, Sister? Tell me."

Sister Teresa was surprised. "What else, Mother? Why, I attend all our religious services, teach my lessons, and help out at the local primary school. When I have time, I also visit the sick and poor in the slums…"

"My dear Sister!" interrupted Mother Cenacle. "Stop! Don't you know why I have asked to see you? You are doing far too much!"

"Too much?" Sister Teresa was shocked. "How can I do too much for God?" she asked.

Mother Cenacle leaned forward over her desk.

"You are a small woman, Sister. You are making yourself ill by taking on too much. How can you serve God if you are not well?"

Sister Teresa bowed her head. "I'm sorry, Mother Cenacle. I will try to rest more."

"Try? I'm afraid that's not good enough, Sister," the older nun said firmly. "I order you to rest on your bed for three hours every afternoon. This is for your own good, Sister."

Sister Teresa was heartbroken. How could she work for God by lying on her bed? She went to ask the advice of Father Exem, the young priest who guided her prayers.

Father Exem knew Sister Teresa well. He admired her faith and unfailing kindliness. Yet there was something about her he did not quite understand. Although she was slight and frail, she seemed to burn with an inner fire. Sometimes it almost alarmed him.

As she knelt before him asking for advice, Father Exem wasn't quite sure what to say. He couldn't tell her to disobey Mother Cenacle. But he didn't want to stand in God's way either.

Eventually, he said calmly, "When you became a nun, what vows did you take?"

"Poverty, chastity, and obedience, Father."

"Then there's your answer, Sister."

She lifted her head slightly. "I don't understand, Father."

"Obedience, Sister. I'm afraid you must do what Mother Cenacle says."

For the first and only time in her adult life, Sister Teresa broke down in tears.

Calcutta, India, where Sister Teresa worked, was one of the largest and poorest cities in the world. Hundreds of thousands of people were crammed together in slums like Motijhil. Their houses were just flimsy shacks, with no toilets, bathrooms, or running water. The poor had no schools or proper medical services. Many lived and died on the streets.

The Second Call

Rest did not make Sister Teresa better.
Once she was allowed, she worked all the
harder. She became so thin and pale that
Mother Cenacle was worried she might
have to go to the hospital.

Father Exem agreed. The 36-year-old
nun needed a break. He knew Sister Teresa
was worried that she was not doing enough
for the very poor. Perhaps it was because she
lived close to the slum areas of Calcutta?
He decided that she needed a change and
time to recover – away from the heat, bustle,
and poverty of the city.

So, on September 10, 1946, Sister Teresa
was put on a train for Darjeeling, a pleasant
town high in the foothills of the Himalaya
Mountains.

Father Exem and Mother Cenacle thought
that she would return refreshed and ready
to restart her life as a Loreto nun.

They were both completely wrong.

The train was hot and crowded. Sister Teresa looked around her carriage at the mothers struggling with young children, the farmers carrying baskets of chickens, the businessmen, and the holidaymakers. It all seemed so different from the calm of the convent.

After a couple of hours, the train stopped at a station. Beggars dressed only in dirty rags shuffled along the platform asking for money. Flies buzzed around open sores on their bodies. Many of them were deformed. Sister Teresa had nothing to give them but her blessing.

Couldn't I give them more? she wondered.

Then the whistle sounded, the beggars slipped by the window, and the train puffed away into the countryside. Sister Teresa closed her eyes and prayed.

Long ago, when she was just a girl, God had called her to serve him as a nun. Now she felt a second call. Yes, she had to change her life. She must leave the Loreto order and devote herself to the service of the poorest of the poor.

She knew it was God's will.

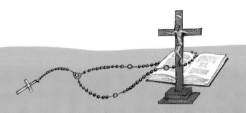

India was part of the British Empire in 1946. But the British had agreed that it would become an independent country the next year. India's millions of Muslims did not want to be part of an independent India. They wanted a country of their own, Pakistan. While this problem was being sorted out, there was fighting between Muslims and Hindus. This conflict, which Sister Teresa saw, made life in Calcutta even harder.

Wait!

Father Fallon cleared the altar and looked around the chapel before switching off the lights. He almost missed the tiny figure kneeling in the shadows at the back.

But, although he couldn't see the nun's face, he recognized her at once.

Father Fallon had served the Darjeeling
convent for years. He kept a kindly eye on the
nuns, ready to help with any difficulties. Now,
it seemed that Sister Teresa needed his help.
She rarely spoke, spent long hours at prayer,
and made private notes on scraps of paper.

When Sister Teresa rose to leave, Father
Fallon called to her gently. "Sister Teresa?"

"Yes, Father?" She approached him, her
head bowed.

"You seem very wrapped up in something, Sister," Father Fallon said gently.

"Indeed I am, Father."

"Is everything all right? Are you happy?"

Sister Teresa raised her head. The priest wished he hadn't spoken. He had never seen a face so bright, so radiant with joy.

"Happy?" she smiled. "Yes, thank you, Father. I have never been happier in my life!"

Father Fallon asked no more questions. Sister Teresa, he decided, had no need of help from him or anyone else.

When Sister Teresa returned to Calcutta, everyone noticed a change in her. She was more peaceful and smiled more than ever.

Father Exem was pleased. It seemed that Sister Teresa's stay in Darjeeling had been just what she had needed.

"I am glad to see you so well, Sister," he said, smiling widely. "I imagine you now see your life here differently?"

"Yes, Father. I do."

"And you look forward to returning to your work in the school?"

Sister Teresa gave him a strange look.

"Maybe, Father," she said. "But first, would you read these and give me your advice?" She handed him the notes she had made.

Father Exem took the notes home and studied them. They set out Sister Teresa's belief that God had called her to leave the Loreto order. She would keep her vows and form a group of Sisters devoted to serving the poorest of the poor in the slums.

Father Exem was not entirely surprised.

"You must realize that you have chosen a very difficult path, Sister," he told her solemnly when they next met.

Sister Teresa nodded.

Father Exem continued. "You will need the permission of the Mother Superior of the Loreto Order, the Archbishop of Calcutta, and, finally, His Holiness the Pope. Are you prepared for all this?"

Sister Teresa showed no alarm. "I am, Father."

"And you're certain that God has called you to work with the very poorest?"

"I am, Father."

Father Exem nodded. "Then I suggest you wait. If, after a year, you are still certain of God's calling, we'll see what we can do"

Sister Teresa smiled. "Thank you, Father. God bless you!"

The head of the Roman Catholic Church is an elected Pope. Each country has one or more archbishops, who look after church matters in their region. No one can set up a new order of monks or nuns without the Pope's permission. But first they need the support of their local archbishop.

You May Leave!

Archbishop Périer of Calcutta was a wise but strict man. He was not pleased when he heard that a nun wanted to leave her order and work on her own.

"My dear Father Exem, what is she thinking of?" he exclaimed.

"She says it's the will of God, Your Grace," Father Exem replied nervously.

The Archbishop sat back in his chair. "No one can be sure of the will of God – not me, not you, and almost certainly not Sister Teresa. And what *is* this work that she wants to do?"

"She wants to live and work with the poor, Your Grace," replied Father Exem.

"We have plenty of orders working with the poor. One more will only confuse things."

Father Exem did not give up. "Your Grace, Sister Teresa wants to work with those who have no helpers – the poorest of the poor, the homeless, the sick, the lonely, the dying."

It was as if the words
had touched the Archbishop's
heart. He stood up and went over
to the cross hanging above his desk.
For a few moments he gazed at it,
lost in thought. Then he turned back
to Father Exem.

"Well, Father," he said slowly,
"this Sister Teresa seems to have
convinced you. I won't turn
her down, but we must wait.
God moves in mysterious
ways, Father. Very mysterious
ways, sometimes."

Sister Teresa was not good at waiting.
She wanted to start her new work immediately
and bombarded Father Exem with letters.
She also asked him to return to the Archbishop
several times. On each occasion the reply was
the same: wait.

The Archbishop sent Sister Teresa away from Calcutta a second time so she could think things over.

Still the letters came. When the Archbishop became seriously ill, Sister Teresa wrote to say that she would pray for him. If he recovered, she suggested, perhaps it would be a sign that God was on her side? The Archbishop did recover, but he remained unmoved.

In the end, though, the waiting was over.

Archbishop Périer finally became sure that Sister Teresa was guided by the will of God.

The Mother Superior of the Loreto Order agreed to let her go. All that was needed now was permission from the Pope.

In the spring of 1948, Father Exem asked to see Sister Teresa one Sunday morning before breakfast. Seeing him holding a large envelope, she asked to go away and pray. When she returned, a few moments later, Father Exem gave her the good news.

"His Holiness the Pope has agreed to your request, Sister," he said. "You can do your work. You are no longer a Loreto nun."

Without hesitating, Sister Teresa replied, 'Father, can I go to the slums now?'

Roman Catholic nuns all belong to one of the many orders. These are communities of nuns, each with its own aim and lifestyle. The Loreto Order was set up in the nineteenth century, and its members teach in schools all over the world. The headquarters, where Sister Teresa received her first training, is in Ireland.

Pray

Sister Teresa was not allowed to leave the convent until everything was in order.

It wasn't easy. Many nuns were upset that one of their favorites had chosen to leave them. Mother Cenacle broke down in tears. Mother Ita, the convent's Mother Superior, was so shocked she went to bed for a week.

But, the nuns helped Sister Teresa in the best way they knew — by asking for God's help and guidance. A notice on the convent board read, "Do not criticize. Do not praise. Pray."

Sister Teresa decided that the black clothes of the Loreto nuns were unsuitable for working in the slums. They would set her apart from ordinary people. Wandering through the local bazaar, she saw a cheap white sari with three blue stripes round the edge. She decided that this was what the new order would wear. She bought three saris so she would always have a clean one to wear.

Father Exem and the Archbishop were still not ready to let Sister Teresa start work. To help the poor properly, they agreed, she needed medical knowledge. So, in August, she was sent to the Patna Medical Centre to take a nursing course.

The training, led by Sister Stephanie, was supposed to last at least six months. But that was far too long for Sister Teresa. After a few weeks, she wrote to Father Exem, asking for permission to leave. Confused, he went to Patna to see what was going on.

The visit was full of surprises. First, he did not recognize Sister Teresa in her sari. Then, Sister Stephanie assured him that her pupil knew all that she needed.

Father Exem looked flustered. "But what if she makes a mistake?" he asked.

"Father," Sister Stephanie replied firmly, "Sister Teresa won't make mistakes."

The traditional nuns' dress, or habit, in the 1940s had hardly changed since medieval times. It was a long, loose black dress and a white or black headdress. Only the nuns' feet, hands, and face were visible. Sister Teresa's decision to swap this dress for an Indian sari shocked many people.

A Missionary of Charity

Sister Teresa woke up, washed, and said her
prayers. She then sat thinking for a few
minutes. This was it. The moment she had
been waiting for since God spoke to her on
the train to Darjeeling. Her mission to the
poorest of the poor was about to begin.

In some ways it was quite frightening.
She was alone, with no money, and only a
little food. Her home was this one small room.

Outside lay the sprawling chaos of the
Motijhil slum, with its disease, poverty,
and crime.

But the people of the Motijhil were God's
people, Sister Teresa told herself. He loved
them as much as the rich – perhaps even
more. And he had chosen her to help them.

No, she was not afraid. God was at her side.

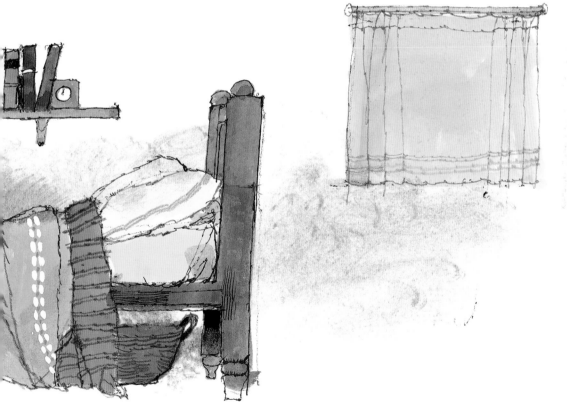

After breakfast, Sister Teresa opened the door and stepped outside. The narrow street was littered with garbage of every kind. The smell of smoke, scent, and decay hung in the clammy air.

A whirlwind of noise surrounded her –
shouting, groaning, ringing, clattering, singing.
Sister Teresa smiled to herself. This is where
I belong, she thought happily.

She was already known to some of the Motijhil children. When they saw her, they ran up laughing.

"Welcome, Ma! Why are you here, Ma? Tell me a story, Ma!" Their eager chattering brought fresh joy to her heart.

When a crowd of about 20 children had gathered, she led them to a piece of wasteland. Here she squatted down and began to teach. The children had never had a day's schooling in their lives. They sat spellbound, watching as she drew letters in the dirt with a piece of stick. When the time came for her to go, they begged her to return.

"Every day, Ma!" called out Gupta, a little boy of no more than four. "Please come every day!"

Sister Teresa hugged him. "Yes, Gupta. From now on, Ma will be here every day. I promise."

Returning home, Sister Teresa noticed
a woman lying in the gutter on the other side
of the road. She was almost naked. Her skin
was cracked like old paper and part of one leg
had been eaten away. Clearly, she was dying.

Sister Teresa crossed the road and took
the woman's hand.

"God bless you, my dear," she said softly,
lifting the woman's head and cradling it in
her lap. "Soon, all will be well," she whispered,
stroking the wispy hair. "All will be well."

The woman opened her eyes. A broken
smile spread across her lips. "My friend!"
she croaked. "I have a friend!"

Still smiling, she closed her eyes and fell
into a sleep from which she never awoke.

Sister Teresa originally planned to live exactly like the poor
people she was helping, eating only rice and salt. But Sister
Stephanie explained that this would not give her enough
energy – she might become ill. So Sister Teresa insisted that she
and those who worked with her always ate proper meals.

The Beginning

The next morning, Sister Teresa walked the same streets. The body of the woman who had died in her arms had been removed. But, before she reached her open-air classroom, she came across others dying in dreadful loneliness.

Not wanting to let down her pupils, she had to leave them. But she promised herself that she would return.

Twice as many boys and girls as yesterday had gathered to greet her. Before lessons began, she got them to sweep the space on which they sat. Then she sent them all off to wash at the nearest pump.

Tiny Gupta was disappointed. "Why are we washing when it is school time, Ma?" he asked.

Sister Teresa waited until everyone had sat down, then explained. "School is not just about letters and numbers, children. First, you must learn to keep healthy. Washing helps to keep away sickness.  Can children learn when they are sick?"

"No, Ma!" chorused the class.

"Very well, then," announced Sister Teresa, smiling around at her class. "Now that we are clean, we can start our lessons."

Day after day, Sister Teresa returned to teach the young and to comfort the dying of the Motijhil. It was hard, terribly hard. But never once did she think that God had forgotten her.

When word of what was happening spread around the city, other nuns came to help. Some of them were pupils Sister Teresa had taught as a Loreto nun. Gifts of money and food were given, too. Before long, the nuns were able to rent two buildings. One served as a schoolroom, the other as a resting place for the dying poor.

At last, out of tears and prayers and countless kindnesses, Sister Teresa's Missionaries of Charity had been born.

The Pope gave permission in 1950 for Sister Teresa's nuns to become a new order, the Missionaries of Charity. Sister Teresa, as their head, became Mother Teresa. To the usual vows of poverty, chastity, and obedience, she added another: "to give wholehearted free service to the very poorest."

The Missionaries Of Charity

In 1952, the first Home for the Dying was opened in Calcutta, to look after those who had no one to care for them. In 1985, Mother Teresa opened the first hospice for AIDS victims. Now, there are hundreds of places all over the world where the Missionaries of Charity comfort the poor, the dying, and the unwanted.

Sainthood

If it is suggested that someone is canonized, or becomes a saint, the Roman Catholic Church usually waits five years before starting the process.

But in 1999, the Pope announced that they would not wait five years, but would start to look for evidence of Mother Teresa's sainthood at once. She may be the first saint of the new millennium.

Timeline

1910 August 27   Agnes Gonxha Bojaxhiu is born
in Skopje, Albania.

1928   Agnes enters the Order of the Sisters
of Our Lady of Loreto in Ireland and
becomes Sister Teresa.

1931   Sister Teresa is sent to Calcutta in
India to teach English.

1937   Sister Teresa takes her final vows.

1946   On her way to Darjeeling to rest,
Sister Teresa receives another call from
God, to care for the poor and needy.

1948   She leaves the Loreto nuns to work
alone in the slums of Calcutta.

1950   Sister Teresa becomes Mother Teresa
of The Missionaries of Charity, her
own order.

1971   Mother Teresa is awarded the Pope
John Paul XXIII Peace Prize.

1979   She is awarded the Nobel Peace Prize.

1997 Sept 5   Mother Teresa dies.

1999   The Pope announces that Mother
Teresa may become a saint.

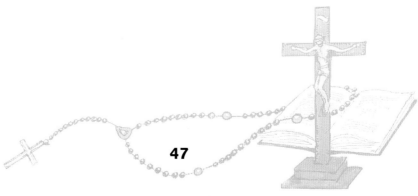

More information

Books to read
Lives and Times: Mother Teresa by
John Barraclough, Heinemann 2000.
Livewire Real Lives: Mother Teresa,
by Iris Howden, Hodder &
Stoughton 1998.
Mother Teresa by Haydn Middleton,
Heinemann 2000.

Famous Lives: Mother Teresa by
Nina Morgan, Hodder Wayland 1998.

Websites
http://www.tisv.be/mt/indmt.htm
http://almaz.com/nobel/peace/
1979a.html

Glossary

convent A religious community
where nuns live.

habit The dress worn by a nun.

mission A goal that someone
wants to achieve.

nun A member of a group of
women following religious vows.

order A group of nuns or monks
who promise to serve God.

Pope The head of the Roman
Catholic Church.

prayers Words said to God.

Roman Catholic The part of
the Christian Church that has the
Pope as its head.

slum A rundown area where
very poor people live.

vows Promises.

Index